The Christmas Tree Advent

4 Christmas Advent Lessons
Thanksgiving and New Year's Bonus Lessons

Building Foundations: A Spirit Filled Children's Church Curriculum

Pastor Tamera Kraft
Revival Fire 4 Kids Resource

Mt Zion Ridge Press
http://mtzionridgepress.com
Managing Editors: Michelle L. Levigne and Tamera Lynn Kraft
Cover Art: Tamera Lynn Kraft

Registration and Digital Files (Available for FREE with purchase of the curriculum): Digital files (jpeg graphics and other resources) are available to anyone who purchases and registers this curriculum at no additional cost. To register, click on this link http://eepurl.com/glsELH or type it in the address box on your browser and fill out the form. We never sell or give away any information we receive.

Or you can insert this QRL Code:

The Christmas Tree Advent is a 4-lesson curriculum about Christmas. Bonus Lessons for Thanksgiving and New Year's are included making it a total of 6 lessons. *The Christmas Tree Advent* is available in PDF download and print.

All Scripture in this curriculum is from the NIV (2011) Bible unless otherwise designated.

THE HOLY BIBLE, NEW INTERNATIONAL VERSION®, NIV® Copyright © 1973, 1978, 1984, 2011 by Biblica, Inc.® Used by permission. All rights reserved worldwide.

Some Scripture is also used from these versions:

THE HOLY BIBLE, INTERNATIONAL CHILDREN'S BIBLE® ICB Copyright© 1986, 1988, 1999, 2015 by Tommy Nelson™, a division of Thomas Nelson. Thomas Nelson is a registered trademark of HarperCollins Christian Publishing, Inc.

NEW KING JAMES VERSION® NKJV® Scripture taken from the New King James Version®. Copyright © 1982 by Thomas Nelson. Used by permission. All rights reserved.

Holy Bible, New Living Translation, Copyright © 1996, 2004, 2015 by Tyndale House Foundation. Used by permission of Tyndale House Publishers, Inc., Carol Stream, Illinois 60188. All rights reserved.

For questions about copyright issues or other matter concerning rights for this curriculum, contact revivalfire4kids@att.net.

Building Foundations Curriculum is a Revival Fire for Kids resource. For more information about Revival Fire for Kids, check out their website at http://revivalfire4kids.net

Materials included:

The Christmas Tree Advent: 4 complete lessons with downloadable media and graphics. Lessons, graphics, videos, and Family Devotion Handouts will be available for immediate download upon registering this curriculum at this link: http://eepurl.com/gIsELH.

Thanksgiving Bonus Lesson – Let's Be Thankful: 1 complete lesson with downloadable media and graphics. Lessons, graphics, videos, and Family Devotion Handouts will be available for immediate download upon registering this curriculum at this link: http://eepurl.com/gIsELH.

New Year's Bonus Lesson – Chosen By God for a Purpose: 1 complete lesson with downloadable media and graphics. Lessons, graphics, videos, and Family Devotion Handouts will be available for immediate download upon registering this curriculum at this link: http://eepurl.com/gIsELH.

How To Use This Curriculum:

Scriptural Premise: The first advent (coming) of Jesus gave us Hope, Peace, Joy, and Light. We still have those things today when we accept Christ into our lives.

Decorations: During the first lesson, you will provide an advent wreath. Optionally, Children can create an advent wreath as a craft project. Each lesson will have an activity to decorate a Christmas Tree. You will need various decorations such as the tree, lights, an angel topper, and ornaments. A nativity scene under the Christmas tree is a bonus.

Italics: Italics are used for Scripture. They are also used in this curriculum for passages or speeches the teacher or worker may want to say in their own words. For skits, italics are only used to designate the person speaking.

Welcome:

Welcome: Each lesson will welcome the children with an introduction to that day's message.

Prayer: It's important to start each lesson with prayer.

Rules: A list of 5 Ups are included in the graphics available after registration. Rehearse the rules every week.

Memory Verse: Every lesson has a memory verse. The verse will be included in a slide and will be illustrated in two ways. You can choose to use any of these illustrations to teach the verse, or you could use all three throughout your lesson.

Memory Verse Talk: This is a short talk explaining what the verse means to the children. Memorizing God's Word is important, but it's more important for your students to know what a verse means.

Memory Verse Activity: Children learn by seeing, reading, hearing, and doing. The memory verse activity is a simple tool to help students remember the verse.

Game Time: A Game Time slide is included with registration for this curriculum. It isn't necessary to include a game with every week's lesson, but if you do, you should have a fun game that relates to the lessons. Game Time is the place for that. You may also want to save the game for last so, if the adult service runs long, you can play games until the parents arrive to retrieve their children.

Decoration Activity: Each Christmas lesson will have an activity to decorate a Christmas Tree. You will need various decorations such as the tree, lights, an angel topper, and ornaments. A nativity scene under the Christmas tree is a bonus.

Craft: Some lessons will have a craft activity to go along with the lesson or decorations.

Benevolence: Each Christmas lesson will have time assigned for a benevolence project for your children's ministry. It is suggested you have a benevolence project to get students involved in reaching out to the community. Christmas is a great time to start this.

Praise and Worship: Each week, a time of praise and worship is included to ready the students' hearts to hear the Word of God. It is appropriate to sing Christian Christmas carols during this time. A suggestion for a classic Christmas carol in in each lesson. This curriculum does not provide music because every church has different musical needs, but we recommend ***Bethel Music Kids Christmas Party Album*** available at Apple Music and other suppliers.

Lesson of the Week:

Advent Object Lesson: Each lesson has an object lesson to illustrate the Advent theme for that week.

Bible Story: Each week, a Bible story is included to go with the lesson.

Object Lessons: At least two object lessons illustrate the points of each week's lesson. Resources for the object lessons are not included but are readily available at most local stores.

Message: A short message ties up the lesson for the day and asks for a response from the students.

Home Application: Each lesson will include a handout for the children to take home. Each handout will include this week's memory verse, a summary of the lesson, a Bible reading for each day, and a weekly family activity. This handout is available as a printable PDF download upon registration of this curriculum. This will be a helpful guide for parents who have family devotions.

Registration and Digital Files (Available for FREE with purchase of the curriculum): Digital files (JPEG graphics, other resources) are available to anyone who purchases and registers this curriculum at no additional cost. To register, click on this link: http://eepurl.com/glsELH or type it in the address box on your browser and fill out the form. We never sell or give away any information we receive.

Or you can insert this QRL Code:

Thanksgiving Bonus Lesson

Let's Be Thankful

Psalm 95:2 (NKJV) *Let us come before His presence with thanksgiving; Let us shout joyfully to Him with psalms.*

The Christmas Tree Advent Lessons

Jesus is Our Hope

Matthew 1:21 (NIV) *She will give birth to a son, and you are to give him the name Jesus, because he will save his people from their sins.*

Jesus is Our Peace

Isaiah 9:6 (NIV): *For to us a child is born, to us a son is given, and the government will be on his shoulders. And he will be called Wonderful Counselor, Mighty God, Everlasting Father, Prince of Peace.*

Jesus is Our Joy

Matthew 2:10 NIV: *When they saw the star, they were overjoyed.*

Jesus is Our Light

Luke 2:32 (NLT): *He is a light to reveal God to the nations, and he is the glory of your people Israel!*

New Year's Bonus Lesson

Chosen by God for a Purpose

Jeremiah 29:11 (NIV): *For I know the plans I have for you," declares the Lord, "plans to prosper you and not to harm you, plans to give you hope and a future.*

TABLE OF CONTENTS

Bonus Thanksgiving Lesson – Let's Be Thankful

Focus Point: We should always be thankful to God, not just on Thanksgiving

Goal: Students will learn to show thanks to God all year long.

Verse of the Day: Psalm 95:2 (NKJV) *Let us come before His presence with thanksgiving; Let us shout joyfully to Him with psalms.*

Supplies Needed:

- donuts or mini pies
- blindfolds
- table and chairs
- wet wipes
- bean bag or beach ball
- thank-you note
- Rubbermaid or another brand of plastic containers
- donut for additional object lesson
- calendar with Thanksgiving circled
- cardstock
- ink blotter or paint
- hand wipes

Opening: (use Thanksgiving Opening Slide. - Available free with registration of this curriculum.)

Welcome:

What day is this coming Thursday? Allow the children to answer. *What are some of the things we do on Thanksgiving?* Allow the children to answer. *The most important reason for Thanksgiving, and the reason it was created, was to remind us to be thankful to God for everything He has done for us.*

Prayer: Ask a child to pray over the service.

Rules: (use Thanksgiving 5 Ups slide) Go over 5 Up rules.

Go over the *5 Ups Rules*: 1. Sit up straight. 2. Listen up. 3. Hush up. 4. Don't get up and run around or go to the bathroom. 5. Worship Up! (stand up and participate during praise and worship)

Activity Songs: Choose one or two fast-moving activity songs about being thankful.

Game Time: Thanksgiving Food (use game time slide)

Supplies Needed: donuts or mini pies, blindfolds, table, chairs, wet wipes

Have a couple of donuts or a mini pie sitting on a table for each student participating. The student sits on a chair in front of the donut. Explain this is a food eating contest. The first student to eat the donuts/pie wins. But there is a catch. Each student is blindfolded and can't use his hands. Blindfold the students and tell them when to start. Play fast-moving music while they try to eat their food blindfolded and without using their hands. If you have older students and want to make this game more difficult, you can move the donuts away from them once they are blindfolded.

One of my favorite things to do on Thanksgiving is eat. Eating all those good foods is a lot of fun, but the most important thing we can do on Thanksgiving is to thank God for His many blessings.

Offering: Freely Give

Matthew 10:8 (NIV) says, "Freely you have received; freely give." Because God has given us so much, we shouldn't have a problem with freely giving in the offering. That is one way we can show thanks to God.

Verse of the Day: Psalm 95:2 (NKJV) *Let us come before His presence with thanksgiving; Let us shout joyfully to Him with psalms.*

Memory Verse Talk: Thanksgiving Joy (use Let's Give Thanks, slide A)

Have you ever thought that giving thanks could cause you to be happy? This Scripture says that when we come into God's presence with thanksgiving, we can shout joyfully. I don't know about you, but I don't shout joyfully unless I'm happy, very happy.

They've even done a study on what makes people happy. According to Harvard Health, *thankful people are much happier than unthankful people. One reason for this is thankfulness changes the brain to create more positive thoughts. I could have told them that because of this verse. The question is, "Do you want to be happy?" If you do, then start thanking God and other people all year long.*

Memory Verse Activity: Thanksgiving Beanbag

Supplies needed: bean bag or beach ball (You will use this bean bag later in the lesson.)

Have the students stand in the center. Explain that you will have them throw the beanbag to each other. If a student catches the beanbag, he has to say the next word in the memory verse. Repeat this a few times until the students know the verse by heart. Then have your students say the whole verse if they catch the bean bag.

Bible Story: Ten Lepers

(Luke 17:12-19)

Supplies needed: thank-you note

Preparation: Choose eleven students to act out this story. If you have a smaller children's ministry, you can use fewer students represent the ten lepers. If needed, you could have as few as two students represent the lepers.

Have you ever given someone a gift? Normally, when someone receives a gift, he or she will thank the person who gave the gift. Sometimes in person, sometimes through text or email, and occasionally by sending one of these. Show thank-you note. *Before text and emails, everyone thanked each other in person or by sending a thank-you note. We still send out thank-you notes for special occasions like baby showers, weddings, and birthday parties. Some people never thank the person who gave them the gift. They never send texts or emails. They never say thank-you in person, and they never send a thank-you note. What would you think of someone who never thanks anyone?* Allow students to answer

If someone doesn't thank me, I think that person is ungrateful for what I've done. It isn't a nice feeling, but it happens to everyone. It even happened to Jesus.

Have ten students stand on the left side of you and one student representing Jesus stand on the right. As you tell the story, have the students act it out.

Ten men came to Jesus and begged Him to heal them. They cried, "Jesus, have pity on us!" Have the ten students on your left approach the student representing Jesus and say, "Jesus, have pity on us!"

These men were desperate. They had a skin disease called leprosy. This disease ate away their skin. It was contagious, meaning everyone who had it could spread it to other people, a little like Covid, and it had no cure. Nobody wanted to catch leprosy, so a law was enacted. It wasn't like today where anyone with Covid has to wear a mask. These people had to live in a leprosy village outside of the city. If they did leave, they couldn't approach anyone. In fact, they had to yell, "unclean," wherever they went so people would know to stay away from them.

Have the ten students yell, "Unclean."

Because of that, these men were breaking the law by approaching Jesus. Jesus knew this, but He had compassion on them. He told them to go to the priest who would check them and see if they still had leprosy. The men went on their way.

Have the students walk away together. *As they were on their way, Jesus healed them.* Have the students shout for joy.

Nine of the former lepers went on their way. Have these students take their seats.

But one of the men came back to Jesus and thanked Him. Have the one student come back and thank Jesus, then have both students take their seats.

Jesus was amazed that only one leper was thankful enough to thank Him. That still is true today. God does so much for us. Even if He never did anything else, He saved us from our sins. I don't want to be one of those people who never thank Him.

Beanbag of Thanksgiving:

Supplies needed: beanbag or beach ball

Explain to the students that you will throw the beanbag to each of them. When they catch the beanbag, they will have to name something they are grateful for. Give each child the opportunity.

When you are finished, throw the beanbag into the air. After you catch it, tell your students you are grateful for them because the Bible says children are a reward from the Lord, so your students are your reward.

Praise and Worship: Choose a couple of fast songs and a slow song to lead children into praise and worship. Before you start, tell your students that one way to show thankfulness to God is by praising and worshipping Him with songs.

Story of Thanksgiving:

(use Let's Give Thanks slides B-C)

Since Thanksgiving is an American holiday, it is good to teach students the real story of Thanksgiving. Because it is a Christian holiday, it tends to get distorted by the schools. Even Christian schools sometimes don't know the whole story.

Start by asking one of your students how Thanksgiving started. Afterward, thank the student and tell him he was mostly right, but many teachers don't know the whole story of Thanksgiving. You're about to tell it now.

Tell this story in your own words.

Show slide B. *Most children are taught that pilgrims came to America to flee religious persecution. That's not exactly true. Pilgrims and Puritans were persecuted for believing that Christians could have a personal relationship with Jesus separate from the Church of England. But they traveled to Holland to flee the persecution, not America.*

So why did they travel to America? There were many reasons, but the main reason is they felt compelled by God to come to America and establish a colony of people who honored God. Many called this colony, New Jerusalem, believing that God had established this new land to spread the gospel to the world. William Bradford wrote in his journal that the motivation came from "a great hope for advancing the kingdom of Christ."

Pilgrims and Puritans were not the same. Pilgrims believed they should separate themselves from the Church of England and the world systems. Puritans believed in working within the system. When they came to America, Puritans wished to set up the government so that religious freedom of expression would be established. Pilgrims wanted freedom of religion so they were free to worship without fear of persecution. Both Pilgrims and Puritans wanted freedom of religion to protect the church from the government, not to protect the government from the church.

Show slide C. *Many schools teach that Thanksgiving was a secular festivity to celebrate the colony surviving and harvesting their first crop. But letters written by the Pilgrims tell a different story. God was such a part of their everyday life that they included God in everything. One such letter states that Thanksgiving was a celebration so that "God be praised" for what He had brought them through.*

John Winthrop called New England a City on a Hill in one of his sermons. He, as well as many other Puritans and Pilgrims, believed they had made a covenant with God to be a new nation that was a model of Christianity to the world. William Bradford believed that America was called to spread the gospel to the world. Since the Pilgrims and Puritans came to America, the United States of America has sent missionaries to more nations and more remote places in the world than any other nation on Earth. Could it be they were right?

Object Lessons:

1. No Left-Over Thanks

Supplies needed: Rubbermaid or another brand of food storage container

What are some of the things your family will eat for Thanksgiving dinner? Have the students answer.

Which are your favorites? Have the students answer.

How many of you have some of these containers in your refrigerator? Have the students answer.

What happens if some of the food during the Thanksgiving dinner is left over? Have the students answer.

Show plastic containers.

I always have lots of leftovers after Thanksgiving. Name some leftovers you might have.

There's one thing I don't have leftovers of at Thanksgiving, though. Thanksgiving is a day set aside to thank God for His blessings. But we shouldn't give God thanks only on Thanksgiving. When we do that, it's like serving God leftover thanks. We should thank God every day for His blessings.

2. Looking at the donut or the hole

Supplies needed: a donut

Last Thanksgiving was awful. I hope this one is better. You may be wondering what was so awful. Well, I was invited to someone else's house, so I didn't have to cook. Wait a minute. I guess that was good, not awful.

Anyway, I went there for dinner, and my favorite part of the turkey is the drumstick. There were only two drumsticks, and before they passed the platter to me, someone else took both drumsticks. I did eat a thigh, and wing, and a breast, but I really wanted those drumsticks. I guess it wasn't that bad. The meat was so tender and juicy. I don't think I've ever eaten a turkey I liked better.

But then, those mashed potatoes. They were good, really good, but I don't like that much butter on my mashed potatoes. And they had green beans for a vegetable. They should have known my favorite vegetable is broccoli. Not only that, they served cornbread stuffing. I like white bread stuffing.

The worst part was the dessert. Apple pie is my favorite, and they had pumpkin pie. I like pumpkin pie, but I like apple pie better.

If I came to your house for Thanksgiving and complained about a food dish your parents served me, what would you think?

Let the students answer. If nobody says it, suggest "ungrateful."

You'd be right. I didn't really have a bad Thanksgiving, but if I had an ungrateful attitude like that, I would have had an awful Thanksgiving even with all that great food.

Show the donut. *Sometimes, it's all how you look at things. I could look at this donut and see a delicious treat, or I could look at it and focus only on the hole. If I focus on the donut, I'm happy and thankful. If I focus on the hole, I won't see the great-tasting donut, and I'll make myself miserable and ungrateful.*

Even when things seem bad, we can find reasons to be thankful. I'll give you one example. Suppose your parents don't have the money to buy a huge Thanksgiving dinner, but they do give you good food to eat. You can still be thankful. Some kids don't have enough to eat.

Over the next week, when something goes wrong, try to find the donut around the hole. Look for something to be thankful for.

Message: Reasons to Thank God

Supplies needed: calendar with Thanksgiving circled

This is a calendar, and it has Thanksgiving circled. Many people believe we should thank God on Thanksgiving, and they're right. Thanksgiving is a day we set apart to thank God, and that is good to do. But God wants us to thank Him every day.

Talk about each of these reasons we should thank God every day.

God is good, and God's love lasts forever. 1 Chronicles 16:34 (NIV) *Give thanks to the LORD, for he is good; his love endures forever.*

God does great things. Psalm 9:1 (NIV) *I will give thanks to you, LORD, with all my heart; I will tell of all your wonderful deeds.*

Jesus died on the cross to save me from my sin. 1 Corinthians 1:4 (NIV) *I always thank my God for you because of his grace given you in Christ Jesus.*

We can thank God even during bad times. 1 Thessalonians 5:18 (NIV) *Give thanks in all circumstances; for this is the will of God in Christ Jesus for you.*

We can bring all our problems to God in prayer. Philippians 4:6 (NIV) *Do not be anxious about anything, but in every situation, by prayer and petition, with thanksgiving, present your requests to God.*

When we have thankful hearts, God fills us with joy. Psalm 16:11 (NIV) *You make known to me the path of life; you will fill me with joy in your presence, with eternal pleasures at your right hand.*

Response Time:

Encourage the children to come to the front to worship and thank God. Let them know that it is possible God will fill them with joy as they continue to thank Him.

Small Group Activity: Hands of Jesus Cards for Missionaries

Supplies needed: cardstock, ink blotter or paint, hand wipes

Praying for You

Have each student dip a hand on the ink blotter or paint. Make sure the student Have the student write "Praying for You" on top of the sheet. Explain that you are going to mail all of these cards to missionaries your church supports.

The Christmas Tree Advent Lesson 1 - Jesus is Our Hope

Focus Point: Because Jesus was born, we have hope in Him.

Goal: The students will learn it is good and right to celebrate Christ's birth because He gives us hope.

Verse of the Day: Matthew 1:21 (NIV) *She will give birth to a son, and you are to give him the name Jesus, because he will save his people from their sins.*

Supplies Needed:

- supplies for a benevolence project
- Advent wreath
- optional – supplies to make an Advent wreath
- 2 sets of gift tags with each word of the verse on one tag,
- 2 gift bags
- a book about pregnant women, a pair of baby booties or something that symbolizes having a baby
- cardstock or posterboard
- red or green ribbon or yarn
- glue or scotch tape
- scissors
- hole punch
- stickers, glitter, markers, and other items for decorating Advent Calendar

Opening: *Christmas Tree Advent* Slide (Available free with registration of this curriculum.)

Welcome: Advent

Welcome children. For the next four weeks, we're going to celebrate Advent. Advent is a Latin word that means "coming." At Christmas time, we celebrate the first coming of Jesus Christ into the world. In this first Advent, He was born as a baby so He could grow up and provide the way for salvation. But there are three Advents in Scripture. The first happened 2,000 years ago when Jesus came into the world as a baby to live as a man and die for us. The second can happen now. Jesus wants to come into our lives now. The third will happen in the future when Jesus comes back to the world as King of Kings and Lord of Lords.

Prayer: Ask a child to pray over the service.

Rules: (use rules slides) Go over the 5 Ups Rules.

Go over the *5 Ups Rules*: 1. Sit up straight. 2. Listen up. 3. Hush up. 4. Don't get up and run around or go to the bathroom. 5. Worship Up! (stand up and participate during praise and worship)

Theme or Activity Songs: Choose one or two fast-moving activity songs that go with the curriculum.

Benevolence Project:

At Christmastime, it is a great idea to involve your students in a benevolence project. This is the time where you can talk to your students about that project. If your church has a project they are already involved in, find a way to include your students. If not, here are some suggestions for projects:

- Sing at a nursing home.
- Make Christmas cards and collect gifts for missionaries.
- Collect canned goods for a nearby homeless shelter.
- Find out if there is a local project you can participate in.
- Serve food at a nearby soup kitchen.

Optional Decoration Activity: Make a Wreath

There are many craft projects online that describe how to make a wreath with anything from a Styrofoam ring and greenery to modeling clay and birthday candles. If you want to make a wreath with your students instead of buying one, check them out.

Advent Object Lesson: Hope

The wreath should have three purple candles and one pink candle. Some also have a white candle in the middle for a Christmas Eve service. When the wreath is finished, light the first purple candle. *This candle symbolizes hope.*

Talk to the children about what they hope to get for Christmas. Tell them about a gift you hoped to receive when you were a child, but you didn't get it. You got something else instead.

The hope we have in Jesus is completely different. He gives us the hope of salvation. All we have to do is put our hope in Him and accept His free gift of salvation. But He gives us many more free gifts. We can hope in Him for healing, for deliverance, for protection, for boldness, and for the baptism of the Holy Spirit. We have the sure hope that, if we accept His gift of salvation, we will someday live for eternity in Heaven with Him. Why hope for something you can't have? When your hope is in Jesus, you can trust in Him completely.

Verse of the Day: Matthew 1:21 (NIV) *She will give birth to a son, and you are to give him the name Jesus, because he will save his people from their sins.*

Memory Verse Talk: (use *The Christmas Tree Advent* Lesson 1, slide A)

Christmas is a time of hope. Christians have the greatest hope of all because Jesus was born to save us from our sins. Because of that, our hope is found in Him.

Memory Verse Activity: Verse Relay (use *The Christmas Tree Advent Lesson 1*, slide A)

Supplies needed: 2 sets of gift tags with each word of the verse on one tag, 2 gift bags

Split your students into two teams. Each gift bag will hold one set of gift tags with the memory verse written on them. The team who sorts the gift tags so they correctly show the memory verse first, wins.

Object Lesson: Wreaths

Supplies needed: Advent Wreath

Have you ever wondered why wreaths are made in a circle? Why not a square or a triangle, or even a hexagon?

I like to think wreaths are made in circles because the circle symbolizes eternal life. Because Christ came to Earth, we have eternal life in Him. He is our hope, and our hope is in Him. The Bible talks about this hope.

Matthew 12:21 (NIV): *"In his name the nations will put their hope."*

Colossians 1:27 (NIV): *"To them God has chosen to make known among the Gentiles the glorious riches of this mystery, which is Christ in you, the hope of glory."*

The circle can also symbolize God's unending love. We usually hang wreaths on the door to welcome guests just as Jesus welcomes us to have eternal life in Him.

Wreaths can be made out of lots of things and come in many different colors, but did you ever notice Advent wreaths and Christmas wreaths are usually made out of evergreen? Because evergreen trees last all year round, it is a symbol that we have everlasting life in Christ.

We have hope we will live with Jesus forever.

Praise and Worship: Choose a couple of fast songs and a slow song to lead children into praise and worship. It would be good to include a traditional Christmas carol. For this week, we suggest *O Come O Come Emmanuel,* performed by Bethel Kids.

Message/Bible Story: Mary Gets Pregnant

(Matthew 1:18-24; Luke 1:26-38)

Supplies needed: a book about pregnant women, a pair of baby booties, or something that symbolizes having a baby

Tell this story in your own words as you show the object.

When a woman gets pregnant, it means she is having a baby. Every baby who is born has a mother and a father. Sometimes children don't know their fathers, but even then, they have a father somewhere.

When Mary became pregnant, it was different. For the first time in history, a woman became pregnant with a baby who didn't have a father. That's because this child was Jesus, the Son of God. He is our hope who is God with us.

If you have your hope in Jesus and have given your life to Him, even if you don't know your father, or if you don't see your father often, or even if you do have a great earthly father, you have a Heavenly

Father you can put your trust in. Your Heavenly Father is Jesus' Father.

Mary might have been afraid when the angel came and told her what was going to happen. She had a fiancé and was planning to get married. Would Joseph believe her? Even if she was afraid, she showed her hope in God by what she said.

Luke 1:38 Mary said, "I am the servant girl of the Lord. Let this happen to me as you say!" Then the angel went away.

Just as Mary put her hope in God when she was afraid, we can put our hope in God when we're afraid.

When Mary told Joseph, he was confused. He wanted to believe her, but something like this had never happened before. Even though he was confused, his hope was in God. He had a dream that night. An angel appeared to him and told him Mary was telling the truth.

Matthew 1:21 (ICB) She will give birth to a son. You will name the son Jesus. Give him that name because he will save his people from their sins.

Even when we are confused like Joseph, we can put our hope in God. He will never let us down.

That isn't the end of the story. After Jesus was born, died, and rose again, He said He would come back again. We hope for the day He comes again. That is our blessed hope.

Titus 2:13 (NIRV) That's how we should live as we wait for the blessed hope God has given us. We are waiting for Jesus Christ to appear in his glory. He is our great God and Savior.

Let's review.

Just as Mary was pregnant with Jesus, who had a Heavenly Father, we have a Heavenly Father we can put our hope and trust in.

Just as Mary put her hope in God when she was afraid, we can put our hope in God when we're afraid.

Even when we are confused like Joseph, we can put our hope in God. He will never let us down.

We can trust in Jesus to return for us some day. He is our Blessed Hope.

Response Time:

For response time, lay hands on each student and pray for him or her to have hope in God.

Craft Project: Christmas Tree Advent Verses Calendar

Supplies needed: card stock or posterboard for each child, 2 inch strips of red or green ribbon or yarn, 24-inch red or green ribbons or yarn, glue, scissors, scotch tape, hole punch, stickers, glitter, markers, and other items for decorating, templates from The Christmas Tree Advent downloadable media resources

Preparations: Make enough copies of Christmas Tree Background for each child on green cardstock or posterboard. Each tree will require four 8 ½" by 11" pages taped together or one 16" by 20" poster. You can also draw the picture on posterboard. Copy pages of Advent Circles with Verse References for each child, glue, scissors, red yarn or ribbon, hole punch, Christmas sticker, markers, glitter, foam Christmas cut-outs. (Christmas Tree Background and Circles with verses are found in The Christmas Tree Advent media resources.) Cut out the Advent Circles with Verse References. Punch holes in each Circles with Verse References and thread red yarn or ribbon through it. On the opposite side of the circles, number 1-25 with black magic marker. Cut out the Christmas Tree Background. If your students are older and you have plenty of time, you can have them do some of this preparation work. If the first Sunday of your Christmas lessons start after December 1st, you don't need to use the circles for days that have already passed.

Have students glue or tape the Christmas Tree Background on the posterboard or cardstock or have it drawn on the posterboard. Have them glue each ribbon or yarn with a circle onto their Christmas tree so the number shows and the verse reference is on the inside. Punch two holes in the top edge of the posterboard and thread a twenty-four-inch piece of yarn or ribbon through them. Tie the ribbon or yarn together to create a hanger for the poster to be hung on the wall.

Now allow your students to decorate their calendar however they like. Have plenty of decorations available for them to use.

If you prefer, you could also buy an Advent calendar craft from most craft places or from an online store like Oriental Trading.

While the students are decorating their Advent calendars, explain how each verse in their Advent calendar is about the birth or coming of Jesus. They should turn over the circle every day to reveal that day's verse. Then, they can look up the verse references in their Bibles. For younger children, an adult can help them.

The Christmas Tree Advent Lesson 2 – Jesus is Our Peace

Focus Point: Jesus wants us to be at peace.

Goal: Students will learn that because of Jesus, they can have peace inside even when things around them are not peaceful.

Verse of the Day: Isaiah 9:6 (NIV): *For to us a child is born, to us a son is given, and the government will be on his shoulders. And he will be called Wonderful Counselor, Mighty God, Everlasting Father, Prince of Peace.*

Supplies Needed:

- Advent wreath
- Optional craft - Styrofoam balls, Christmas material, scissors, red ribbon, plastic knives
- Christmas tree
- Christmas tree light
- colorful ornaments
- apple ornament or apple

Opening: *Christmas Tree Advent* Slide (Available free with registration of this curriculum.)

Welcome: Advent

Welcome children. Today, we continue celebrating the first coming of Jesus Christ into the world. In this first Advent, He was born as a baby so He could grow up and provide the way for salvation. Even though we don't know the exact day of Jesus' birth, it is right and proper to celebrate this Advent we call Christmas.

During the next Advent, Jesus will return for us and take all the Christians to Heaven to be with Him. We can have peace about this next Advent if we have given our lives to Him.

Prayer: Ask a child to pray over the service.

Rules: (use rules slides) Go over the 5 Ups Rules.

Go over the *5 Ups Rules*: 1. Sit up straight. 2. Listen up. 3. Hush up. 4. Don't get up and run around or go to the bathroom. 5. Worship Up! (stand up and participate during praise and worship)

Theme or Activity Songs: Choose one or two fast-moving activity songs that go with the curriculum.

Benevolence Project:

At this time, have the students work on whatever benevolence project you have decided on.

Optional Craft: Make Christmas Tree Ornaments

Supplies needed: Styrofoam balls, Christmas material, scissors, red ribbon, plastic knives

Preparations: Cut the material in small squares. Cut 4-6-inch strips of ribbon.

Have students poke holes in their Styrofoam balls with their plastic knives. Then have them use the knife to stuff pieces of material in the grooves. When the ball is covered with material, double up the ribbon and stuff it deep into one of the grooves in the ball to hang on a tree. The ribbon should stay in the ball if you stick it deep enough.

Decoration Activity: Christmas Tree

Supplies needed: Christmas tree, lights, ornaments

Preparations: Have the Christmas tree and lights ready for the students to decorate.

This week, students will decorate the tree with ornaments. Make sure the ornaments are a variety of colors. Use non-breakable ornaments if possible. Don't place garland or a topper on the tree yet. Students will do that in future lessons.

Object Lesson: The Christmas Tree

Supplies needed: Christmas tree, apple ornament

Many people decorate during Christmas with Christmas trees. How many of you have a Christmas tree in your house? Have the students answer. *There are many symbols of Christmas that point to the Bible, and the Christmas tree is one of them. The tree itself can represent the tree of life that Jesus came to Earth to restore to us when we accept Christ as our Savior. It can also represent the cross where Jesus died for our sins. We cut down a tree for Christmas just as Christ was cut down for our sins. But we resurrect the tree in our homes just as Christ was resurrected after three days. Also, just as evergreen trees grow all year long and are always green, Jesus came to Earth to give us everlasting life.*

Some people hang apples on their tree because Adam and Eve sinned by eating the apple. Jesus came to Earth to save us from our sins. Others hang red holly on the tree because the red reminds us of the blood Jesus shed to save us from our sins. The ornaments represent that God wants to give us good things just like the gifts we give each other at Christmas. Those good things are salvation, hope, peace, joy, and other blessings.

History of the Christmas Tree:

Many believe the Christmas tree is used because Druids worshipped trees and celebrated the winter solstice, but this is a distortion of history. In your own words, tell your students some of the history of why we use Christmas trees to celebrate Jesus' first Advent. You can use some or all of these historical references to the Christmas Tree.

The Upside Down Fir Tree: During the 7th century, a monk living in Devonshire spent time there preaching the Word of God. He used the triangular shape of the fir tree to teach about the Trinity of the Father, Son, and Holy Spirit. By the 12th century, the fir tree was hung upside down from ceilings in Central Europe as a symbol of Christianity at Christmas time.

Boniface and Thor's Oak: In the 700s A.D., St. Boniface became a missionary to Germany, where he encountered Druids who worshiped trees. To stop their sacrifices at their sacred Donar Oak near

Geismar, St. Boniface chopped the tree down in 725 A.D. With one mighty blow, he felled the massive oak, and as the tree split, a beautiful young fir tree sprang from its center. He told the people that this lovely evergreen, with its branches pointing to heaven, was indeed a holy tree, the tree of the Christ Child, a symbol of His promise of eternal life. He instructed them to carry the evergreen from the wilderness into their homes and to surround it with gifts, symbols of love and kindness.

The Paradise Tree: From the 11th century, religious plays called "Mystery Plays" included the popular *Paradise Play,* depicting the story of the creation of Adam and Eve, their sin, and their banishment from Eden. An evergreen tree was used for this winter festival and decorated with apples symbolizing the forbidden fruit. The play ended with the promise of the coming Savior.

Wafers were also hung from the tree, symbolizing the forgiveness of sins in communion, making it now not just the tree of the knowledge of good and evil but also the tree of life. This resulted in a very old European custom of decorating a fir tree in the home with apples and small white wafers, representing the Holy Eucharist, at Christmas time. These wafers were later replaced by little pieces of pastry cut in the shapes of stars, angels, hearts, flowers, and bells. In some areas, the custom was still to hang the tree upside down.

In addition to the paradise tree, many German Christians set up a Christmas Pyramid, called a Lichstock – a open wooden frame with shelves for figurines of the nativity, covered with evergreen branches and decorated with candy, pastry, candles, and a star. The star represented the star of Bethlehem, the candles represented the light of Christ coming into the world, the evergreens were the symbol of eternal life, and the candy, fruits, and pastries, the goodness of our life in Christ, the fruit of the Spirit, etc. By the 17th century, the Lichstock and the Paradise Tree became merged into the modern Christmas tree.

Luther's Christmas Tree: There is a popular tradition that Martin Luther was walking on a bright snow-covered, star-lit night pondering the birth of Christ. Enthralled by the evergreen trees, the stars, and the landscape, he took a tree inside and put candles on it to represent the majesty he felt surrounding Christ's birth, as Jesus came down from the stars to bring us eternal life.

Verse of the Day: Isaiah 9:6 (NIV): *For to us a child is born, to us a son is given, and the government will be on his shoulders. And he will be called Wonderful Counselor, Mighty God, Everlasting Father, Prince of Peace.*

Memory Verse Talk: (use *The Christmas Tree Advent* Lesson 2, slide A)

Jesus is the Son of God. When He came to Earth and was born, He was still the Son of God on Earth. He is the King of Kings and Lord of Lords. Because He is in control, He is our counselor when we are going through difficulties. No matter what problems we face, He is the Mighty God who is stronger than our problems. He is our Everlasting Father when we don't know where we can turn. And He isn't only our peace in the midst of a storm, He is our Prince of Peace.

Memory Verse Activity: Christmas Say the Verse If... (use *The Christmas Tree Advent Lesson 1,* slide A)

Explain to your students that you will list things that may or may not apply to them. If something applies to them, they must stand and recite the verse, then sit down. Make sure to call out something where everyone can stand at the beginning and the end of this activity.

Here are some things you can call out:

- Anyone who has ever received a Christmas present
- Anyone who has their Christmas tree decorated in their house
- Anyone who has made Christmas cookies with their family
- Anyone who has eaten Christmas cookies
- Anyone who knows all eight of Santa's reindeer by name
- Anyone who has made a present for someone
- Anyone who loves Christmas

Advent Object Lesson: Peace

Light the second purple candle in the Advent Wreath.

Read Isaiah 9:6: *For to us a child is born, to us a son is given, and the government will be on his shoulders. And he will be called Wonderful Counselor, Mighty God, Everlasting Father, Prince of Peace.*

If hope has a different meaning in the Bible than it does in the world, then peace also has a different meaning. Jesus talked a lot about the peace He came to give. His peace isn't the absence of conflict, war, or trials, but it is a calm assurance that Christ is in control even when the world around us is in chaos.

Here are some verses that promise us God's peace that you might want to share with your students.

John 16:33 *I have told you these things, so that in me you may have peace. In this world you will have trouble. But take heart! I have overcome the world.*

Isaiah 26:3 (ICB) *You, Lord, give true peace. You give peace to those who depend on you. You give peace to those who trust you.*

John 14:27 *Peace I leave with you; my peace I give you. I do not give to you as the world gives. Do not let your hearts be troubled and do not be afraid.*

Romans 15:13 *May the God of hope fill you with all joy and peace as you trust in him, so that you may overflow with hope by the power of the Holy Spirit.*

Ask the children what peace is. Talk to the children about how Jesus is called the Prince of Peace. He's not called that because everything becomes peaceful when we get saved. He brings us peace in the midst of our troubles.

Tell a story about a tragedy in your life and how God gave you peace in it when you trusted in Him.

Praise and Worship: Choose a couple of fast songs and a slow song to lead children into praise and worship. It would be good to include a traditional Christmas carol. We suggest *Silent Night*, performed by Bethel Kids.

Message/Bible Story: Christ Is Born

(Luke 2:1-7)

The Christmas Tree Advent Lesson 2, slides B, C, and D

Tell the story about Mary having the baby, Jesus. Emphasize how she didn't have it easy. *This is the nativity scene most people have at Christmas to show when Jesus was born.* Show slide B.

While she was very pregnant, she had to ride miles on a donkey. They faced many hardships along the trail. They couldn't stop and stay in a hotel every night or even take a shower.

Talk to the children about camping outside without a camper or a tent. Talk about the bad things that can happen when you are camping. Talk mostly about inconveniences, not about scary things like wild animals.

Show slide C. *When Mary and Joseph got to Bethlehem, they couldn't even stay at an inn. They had to stay in a smelly old cave. They didn't have barns like today. They kept their animals in caves. She gave birth in a manger filled with straw. A manger is a feeding trough for animals.*

This was where Jesus was born. He is the King of Kings and Lord of Lords, but He was born in a stable.

They didn't have a doctor or a midwife or even Mary's mother there. Neither Mary nor Joseph knew what was going to happen, but they had peace in the midst of it because they trusted God.

Jesus is the Prince of Peace. He can give us peace even when things aren't going well. He came to give us peace with God. How do we feel at peace when everything goes wrong? The Bible tells us how.

Show Slide D. Isaiah 26:3 (ICB) *You, Lord, give true peace. You give peace to those who depend on you. You give peace to those who trust you.*

Response Time

For response time, give the students time to pray at the altar for peace in whatever situation they are in.

The Christmas Tree Advent Lesson 3 – Jesus is Our Joy

Focus Point: Jesus wants to fill us with joy.

Goal: Students will learn that Jesus wants us to celebrate Him, worship Him, and be filled with joy because of Him.

Verse of the Day: Matthew 2:10 NIV: *When they saw the star, they were overjoyed.*

Supplies Needed:

- Angel or star Christmas tree topper
- silver and gold ornaments
- garland or tinsel
- Advent wreath
- silver bell
- small silver bells for each student
- optional craft supplies
- balloon (silver or gold if possible)

Opening: *Christmas Tree Advent* Slide (Available free with registration of this curriculum.)

Welcome:

Welcome children. Talk to the children about how Christmas is a time of great joy. Ask them what makes them joyful at Christmas. *There are other things that cause people to be joyful, like the birth of a baby. At Christmas, we celebrate the birth of a baby. But this baby was different than any other child. Jesus is the Son of God, and He came to Earth to be our Savior. Because of this, He has brought joy to the world.*

Prayer: Ask a child to pray over the service.

Rules: (use rules slides) Go over the 5 Ups Rules.

Go over the *5 Ups Rules*: 1. Sit up straight. 2. Listen up. 3. Hush up. 4. Don't get up and run around or go to the bathroom. 5. Worship Up! (stand up and participate during praise and worship)

Theme or Activity Songs: Choose one or two fast-moving activity songs that go with the curriculum.

Benevolence Project:

At this time, have the students work on whatever benevolence project you have decided on.

Decoration Activity: Christmas Tree Topper

Supplies needed: Christmas tree topper (either angel or star), silver and gold ornaments, garland, or tinsel

This week, place an angel or a star on top of the tree. Ask your students what they place on the top of their trees. Have the students place the silver and gold ornaments, garland, or tinsel on the tree.

Object Lesson: Tinsel and Tops

Supplies needed: Angel or star tree topper, silver ornaments or garland, silver bells, gold ornaments or garland

Point to the tree topper you placed on the tree.

Usually, an angel or a star is on top of a Christmas tree because both were in the sky the night Jesus was born. The angels proclaimed the good news to the shepherds. The star lit the way of the wise men traveling to Bethlehem. When they saw Jesus, they were filled with joy. (Matthew 2:10)

Point to the silver ornaments or garland you used on the tree.

We use silver on the tree because it has two meanings. It symbolizes the star of Bethlehem that the wise men followed. But it also symbolizes shepherds who rang their silver bells in Bible times to help the sheep find their way. When Jesus was born, angels appeared to shepherds so they could worship Jesus as our Great Shepherd. Jesus came to Earth to help us find our way back to God.

Point to the gold ornaments or garland you used on the tree.

We use gold on the tree because of the wise men. They were sometimes called kings because they were rich, but they weren't kings. They came from the East, probably from Persia where Daniel taught the wise men about God. They probably knew to expect the birth of the great king of Israel because of Daniel. They may have been looking for that star for many generations because they knew, when they saw it, that the real King of Kings and Lord of Lords was born. The Bible doesn't say how many of them there were, the number three is from a song, not from the Bible, but they brought three types of gifts to Jesus: gold, frankincense, and myrrh to show Jesus was born a king. He came to this Earth as a baby, but He is the King of Kings and Lord of Lords.

Verse of the Day: Matthew 2:10 NIV: *When they saw the star, they were overjoyed.*

Memory Verse Talk: (use *The Christmas Tree Advent* Lesson 3, slide A)

Why do you think the wise men were overjoyed when they saw the star? Allow the students to answer. *I think they were overjoyed because they understood that Jesus, the Son of God, was born.*

Memory Verse Activity: Ring the Bells (use *The Christmas Tree Advent* Lesson 3, slide A)

Supplies needed: bells, preferably silver

Give each student a small bell. Have them repeat the verse several times. Every time the students say "overjoyed," they should ring the bells, jump up and down, and cheer. Let them get a little crazy with their rejoicing if they want.

The wise men were overjoyed because of Jesus, and we should show how overjoyed we are when we worship Him. Jesus wants us to be joyful when we worship Him.

Advent Object Lesson: Joy

Light the third purple candle in the Advent Wreath.

Read Matthew 2:10 NIV: *When they saw the star, they were overjoyed.*

Jesus wants us to be joyful, not only about His birth, but because He wants to fill Christians with joy.

Read and explain some of these verses.

God wants us to be full of joy while we seek and worship Him. Philippians 4:4 (ICB): *Be full of joy in the Lord always. I will say again, be full of joy.*

When God fills us with joy, He also fills us with His strength. Nehemiah 8:10 (NIV) *"For the joy of the Lord is your strength."*

Praise and Worship: Choose a couple of fast songs and a slow song to lead children into praise and worship. It would be good to include a traditional Christmas carol. We suggest *Joy to the World, performed* by Bethel Kids.

Message/Bible Story: The Visitors

(Matthew 2:2-12; Luke 2:8-20)

Supplies needed: towel and bathrobes or children's Bible costumes, Burger King crowns, 3 Christmas gift bags or boxes wrapped in Christmas paper, doll, silver bells

For these two stories, have the children act them out. If you have enough students, assign shepherds, sheep, angels, Mary, Joseph, and wise men. Whenever you use the words joy, overjoyed, rejoiced, praise, or worship, have all of the children jump up and down, ring their bells, and say, "Praise the Lord."

You can read Luke 2:8-10 and have the children act out the parts as you say them. Here is the Scripture in NIV.

> *And there were shepherds living out in the fields nearby, keeping watch over their flocks at night. An angel of the Lord appeared to them, and the glory of the Lord shone around them, and they were terrified. But the angel said to them, "Do not be afraid. I bring you good news that will cause great joy for all the people. Today in the town of David a Savior has been born to you; he is the Messiah, the Lord. This will be a sign to you: You will find a baby wrapped in cloths and lying in a manger."*

> *Suddenly a great company of the heavenly host appeared with the angel, praising God and saying, "Glory to God in the highest heaven, and on earth peace to those on whom his favor rests."*

> *When the angels had left them and gone into heaven, the shepherds said to one another, "Let's go to Bethlehem and see this thing that has happened, which the Lord has told us about."*

So, they hurried off and found Mary and Joseph, and the baby, who was lying in the manger. When they had seen him, they spread the word concerning what had been told them about this child, and all who heard it were amazed at what the shepherds said to them. But Mary treasured up all these things and pondered them in her heart. The shepherds returned, glorifying and praising God for all the things they had heard and seen, which were just as they had been told."

Let's look again at what the shepherds did when they heard the message about Jesus. First, they hurried to find baby Jesus and worshipped Him. Even today, Jesus wants to be found. His sheep will seek after Him and worship Him.

Next, they shared everything they had seen, the angels, the Messiah as a baby, all of it. I'm sure some were overjoyed Jesus had been born. Others would have made fun of them, but they didn't care.

After they had shared what they had seen, they rejoiced and praised God.

Baby Jesus had other worshippers from the East who came to His house when He was less than two years old. Sometimes, the other visitors were called kings, but they weren't. They were Magi, sometimes known as wise men. We don't know how many of them there were, but they brought three types of gifts: gold, frankincense, myrrh. They had followed a star because they wanted to worship the new King because of Daniel, the prophet, who years earlier was in charge of the wise men of Babylon and might have told them about the coming King. These men might have been the descendants of those wise men. When they followed the star to the house where Jesus was staying, the Bible says they were overjoyed. They bowed down and worshipped Jesus and gave Him their prize possessions.

All the visitors looked for Jesus, were filled with joy when they found Him, and worshipped Him.

Even today, Jesus wants us to seek Him. Blow up the balloon slightly. *How do we seek God?* Allow students to answer. For each right answer, blow the balloon up a little larger.

One of the ways we seek Him is to worship Him. When we seek Jesus and worship Him, He will fill us with joy. Psalm 16:11 (NIV) You make known to me the path of life; you will fill me with joy in your presence, with eternal pleasures at your right hand.

I don't know why anyone would not want to seek God and worship Him when He makes it so fun when we do.

Response Time

For response time, have the students spend some time worshipping Jesus. Pray for each student to be filled with joy.

Craft Project: Angel or Star Christmas Tree Topper

There are many videos and blog posts online showing how to make a tree topper in the shape of the star or an angel using paper plates or construction paper. This craft can be made simply or elaborately, depending on the age and ability of your students and the time you have to devote to this project.

The Christmas Tree Advent Lesson 4 – Jesus is the Light of the World

Focus Point: Jesus is the Light of the World

Goal: Students will learn that Jesus came to Earth, as God, so that we could be saved.

Verse of the Day: Luke 2:32 (NLT): *I have come into the world as a light, so that no one who believes in me should stay in darkness.*

Supplies Needed:

- scissors
- glue or stapler
- strips of construction paper in the following colors: red, green, and white
- marker
- stickers to decorate the strips
- flashlight
- optional – battery-operated candles

Opening: *Christmas Tree Advent* Slide (Available free with registration of this curriculum.)

Welcome: Advent

Welcome children. Today is that last Sunday to celebrate the first coming of Jesus Christ into the world. Are you excited about Christmas? In this first Advent, even though He was born as a baby, at His birth and at every time before and since He is God.

Prayer: Ask a child to pray over the service.

Rules: (use rules slides) Go over the 5 Ups Rules.

Go over the *5 Ups Rules*: 1. Sit up straight. 2. Listen up. 3. Hush up. 4. Don't get up and run around or go to the bathroom. 5. Worship Up! (stand up and participate during praise and worship)

Theme or Activity Songs: Choose one or two fast-moving activity songs that go with the curriculum.

Benevolence Project:

At this time, have the students finish up whatever benevolence project you have decided on.

Verse of the Day: Luke 2:32 (NLT): *I have come into the world as a light, so that no one who believes in me should stay in darkness.*

Memory Verse Talk: (use *The Christmas Tree Advent* Lesson 4, slide A & B)

There is a species of fish called cave fish. They are normal fresh-water fish, but they live in caves where there is no light, only darkness. Once the fish live there for a while, they not only lose their sight, they lose their eyes. They no longer have the ability to see the light. They only see darkness.

Jesus overcomes darkness because He is the light of the world. But we have a choice. We can give our lives to God and become part of His light. Those who decide not to accept Jesus are like cave fish. They not only stay in darkness, they become so used to it, it seems normal. Only giving our lives to Jesus can restore our spiritual sight.

Memory Verse Activity: Joy to the World

Have students sing the memory verse to the tune of *Joy to the World.* Here is how they would sing it. Verse is sung. Italics are the lyrics to *Joy to the World. I (Joy) have (to the) come (world) into (the Lord) the (has) world (come) as a light (let Earth), so that (receive) no one (her king) who believes in me (in every heart) should stay in darkness. (prepare Him Room.)* Luke 2:32 (And Heaven and Nature Sing) Repeat Luke 2:32 for the chorus.

Decoration and Craft Activity: The Colors of Christmas

Supplies needed: scissors, glue or stapler, strips of construction paper in the following colors: red, green, and white, marker, stickers to decorate the strips

This week, students will place a colorful construction paper garland on the tree. Give each student a certain number of strips for the garland. Students will decorate their strips and write their name on them. While they are doing this, teach them what these colors of Christmas symbolize.

Red: Red symbolizes Christ was born on Christmas so He could shed His blood for the sins of the world.

Romans 5:9 *Now that we have been justified by his blood, how much more will we be saved from wrath through him!*

Green: Green is the color of the evergreens that last all year long even through the winter snow. It symbolizes eternal life that Jesus came to give. If we believe in Him, we will have eternal life in Heaven with Jesus.

John 3:16 *For God loved the world so much that he gave his one and only Son, so that everyone who believes in him will not perish but have eternal life.*

White: White symbolizes the purity of Christ. He lived His life on Earth without ever sinning, He cleanses us from our sins when we become His children. Our sins become as white as snow.

Isaiah 1:18 *Come now, and let us reason together, saith the LORD: though your sins be as scarlet, they shall be as white as snow; though they be red like crimson, they shall be as wool.*

When the students are finished decorating their strips, have them loop and attach them to the other loops. Use glue or a stapler to keep the loops closed.

Once the chain is completed, hang it on the tree.

Object Lesson: Light of the World

Supplies needed: flashlight

Use *The Christmas Tree Advent* Lesson 4, slide C

Teach the following in your own words.

Show flashlight. *When it's dark, I always carry this flashlight. It helps me decide which is the right way. It warns me if there is something in my path I might trip over. It also protects me by showing me the dangers ahead, like a bear or a cliff I might tumble over. A flashlight is a great thing to carry around.*

Jesus was born into a dark world. Yet, He is the light of the world. He has always been the light of the world because He always has been God. But He became man for us, so He could shine His light in us even in the greatest darkness.

Jesus is the light of the world. So, if we accept Him, we won't have to live in darkness. John 8:12 (NIV) When Jesus spoke again to the people, he said, "I am the light of the world. Whoever follows me will never walk in darkness, but will have the light of life."

Because Jesus is the light of the world, He is the light in your world. He'll help you decide the right path. He will warn you when something is dangerous to help keep you from temptation. He protects you when dangers are all around.

Jesus does one more amazing thing as the light of the world. He dispels the darkness. Have any of you ever been afraid of the dark when you were younger? The scary shadows lurked everywhere. What was even more scary was what you couldn't see. I was afraid of the dark when I was little, but my mom fixed the problem. She plugged in a night light. It was a small light that didn't shine very brightly. Still, even that little light was enough to get rid of the scary darkness. That's what Jesus does. He doesn't even leave a shadow.

Show Lesson 4, Slide C

Advent Object Lesson: Light of the World

Supplies needed (optional): battery-operated candles

Light the second purple candle in the Advent Wreath.

Optional: Hand each child a candle.

One reason some churches have a candlelight service around Christmas is because Jesus is the Light of the World. We celebrate Him coming to Earth to bring light to every Christian. We celebrate this because He showed us such great love by coming to Earth to die on the cross for us and then He rose again, showing us the light of God cannot be extinguished.

Optional: *As we worship, let's hold up our candles to show Jesus is the light of the world.*

Praise and Worship: Choose a couple of fast songs and a slow song to lead children into praise and worship. It would be good to include a traditional Christmas carol. We suggest *O Holy Night* or *O Come All Ye Faithful,* performed by Bethel Kids.

Message/Bible Story: Christ Is Dedicated

(Luke 2:22-38)

Use *The Christmas Tree Advent* Slides D, E, F, and G.

It is important for your students to know Jesus wasn't just a great man whose birth we celebrate on Christmas. He is God and always has been. Tell this lesson in your own words, but also read the Bible passages so your students will come to understand this isn't just your opinion. It is in the Bible.

Show Lesson 4, slide D. *Jesus is God. He wasn't just some great prophet or teacher, and He didn't become God. He is God and always has been. That's why He is the light of the world. Matthew 1:23 (NIV) "The virgin will conceive and give birth to a son, and they will call him Immanuel" which means "God with us."*

Show Lesson 4, slide E. *Jesus is the light of the world because He created the world. The book of John calls Jesus the Word.* Read John 1:1-5 (NIV). *In the beginning was the Word, and the Word was with God, and the Word was God. He was with God in the beginning. Through him all things were made; without him nothing was made that has been made. In him was life, and that life was the light of all mankind. The light shines in the darkness, and the darkness has not overcome it.*

Show Lesson 4, slide F. *Jesus is the light of the world because He was born into the world so He could save us from our sins. John 3:16-21 (NIV) For God so loved the world that he gave his one and only Son, that whoever believes in him shall not perish but have eternal life. For God did not send his Son into the world to condemn the world, but to save the world through him. Whoever believes in him is not condemned, but whoever does not believe stands condemned already because they have not believed in the name of God's one and only Son. This is the verdict: Light has come into the world, but people loved darkness instead of light because their deeds were evil. Everyone who does evil hates the light, and will not come into the light for fear that their deeds will be exposed. But whoever lives by the truth comes into the light, so that it may be seen plainly that what they have done has been done in the sight of God.*

Show Lesson 4, slide G. *When Mary and Joseph went to the temple to dedicate Jesus to the Lord, God made sure there was someone there to declare Jesus was the light of the world. A priest named Simeon saw the baby. Luke 2:28-32 (NIV) Simeon took him (Jesus) in his arms and praised God, saying: "Sovereign Lord, as you have promised, you may now dismiss your servant in peace. For my eyes have seen your salvation, which you have prepared in the sight of all nations: a light for revelation to the Gentiles, and the glory of your people Israel."*

Simeon knew this because God had revealed it to him. A woman named Anna was also there. When she saw Baby Jesus, she started praising and worshipping God because He had come to save us from our sins.

Response Time

For response time, give the students time to worship Jesus, the light of the world.

Closing

This would be a great time to give your students a present for Christmas.

Bonus New Year's Lesson - Chosen by God for a Purpose

Focus Point: God has a plan and a purpose for each child's life.

Goal: Children will learn that their lives are important to God

Focus Verse: *For I know the plans I have for you," declares the LORD, "plans to prosper you and not to harm you, plans to give you hope and a future.* Jeremiah 29:11

Supplies Needed:

- Program outline
- costume for Professor Confuzed (lab coat, crazy glasses, pocket protector, etc.)
- costume or puppet for Heavenly Agent (trench coat, sunglasses)
- book
- picture of a bus or a bus schedule
- 2 sets of 14 paper cups
- marker
- calendar or planner
- long sheet of paper with writing
- job application

Opening: Use New Year's Opening Slide. (Available free with registration of this curriculum.)

Welcome:

Supplies needed: program outline, costume for skit person

Good morning, boys and girls.

Interrupted by a person in costume...

You're not supposed to come out yet. Didn't you read your program outline?

Skit person apologizes and leaves.

As I was saying children...

A worker comes running in to ask you when is the time to take the offering.

Now is the time to open the service. If you read your program outline, you'll know when to take the offering.

The worker apologizes and leaves.

I'm sorry for all these interruptions, children. I made a plan for how this service would go, (show program outline) *but my workers forgot to look at the program outline to see what the plan is. Christians are sometimes like that. God has a plan for their lives, but they don't bother to find out what that plan is. When you don't follow a plan in Kid's Church, it can cause confusion. When you don't follow God's plan for your life, it will destroy your life. We need to follow the plan.*

Prayer: Ask a child to pray over the service.

Rules: (use New Year's rules slide) Go over the 5 Ups Rules.

Go over the *5 Ups Rules*: 1. Sit up straight. 2. Listen up. 3. Hush up. 4. Don't get up and run around or go to the bathroom. 5. Worship Up! (stand up and participate during praise and worship)

Game Time: Planning a Song

Children, when I count to 3, sing a song as loud as you can. I want each of you to think of a song you want to sing. But don't tell anyone what that song it is. It doesn't matter which song you sing as long as you sing it really loud. 1…2…3. Give children a few seconds to sing. Hopefully it will sound awful.

Why do you think we sounded so bad? Give the children time to answer. *I think we sounded bad because I didn't plan what we were going to sing. Many people go through their lives making a lot of noise that doesn't make sense, because they don't follow God's plan for their lives. If we don't follow God's plan, our plans won't make sense and we will just be making noise.*

Now, let's plan which song we will sing.

Theme or Activity Songs: Choose one or two fast-moving activity songs that go with the curriculum.

Verse of the Day: Jeremiah 29:11 (NIV) *"For I know the plans I have for you," declares the LORD, "plans to prosper you and not to harm you, plans to give you hope and a future."*

Memory Verse Skit: Memory Verse Mission

(use New Year's, slide A and *Mission Impossible* Music)

(may be used as a puppet or live skit)

Heavenly Agent: Hello, boys and girls. I'm Heavenly Agent. Many people plan things in their lives. When they go on vacation, they plan where they are going, how they will get there and where they will stay. Most wives and mothers plan what their families will eat for dinner. Teen-agers and young adults plan for future careers. God also has a plan for each of our lives. This plan came about before we were ever created and is a plan for our good. Please look at the viewing screen. Jeremiah 29:11 (NIV) says *"For I know the plans I have for you," declares the LORD, "plans to prosper you and not to harm you, plans to give you hope and a future."* Your mission, if you decide to accept it, is to find out what God's plan is for your life, to obey Him and to trust Him to carry out His plan in your life. As always, if you have any difficulty carrying out this mission, the Holy Spirit will be there to help you. This Heavenly Agent will return to Heaven in 5 seconds. 5…. 4…. 3…. 2…. 1…. (Puppet/actor disappears.)

Memory Verse Talk: My Plans

Supplies needed: book, picture of a bus or a bus schedule, calendar or planner

I like to read a lot, (show book) *but I've already read all my books. I have decided to go to the library to sign out some books to read. Normally, I would drive to the library, but my car is in the repair shop, so I plan to take the bus. First, I have to have a bus schedule.* (show bus schedule) *Then, I have to find out which bus goes to the library. I also need to find the bus stop nearest to my house. Once I do that, I need to plan when I am going to the library and when I am coming home.* (show calendar or planner) *Next, I need to look at the bus schedule to see when it will pick me up.*

Boy, there sure is a lot of planning that has to be done just to go to the library on a bus. God has done a lot of planning for each of your lives, too. If it takes this much planning to go to the library, imagine how much planning it takes to plan an entire life.

Jeremiah 29:11 (NIV) says "For I know the plans I have for you," declares the LORD, "plans to prosper you and not to harm you, plans to give you hope and a future."

I'm sure glad I have God to make plans for my life. Aren't you?

Memory Verse Activity:

Supplies needed: 2 sets of 14 paper cups, marker

Preparation: Write the following on each set of cups.

- Cup 1: For I
- Cup 2: know the
- Cup 3: plans I
- Cup 4: have for you
- Cup 5: declares
- Cup 6: the Lord
- Cup 7: plans to
- Cup 8: prosper you
- Cup 9: and not to
- Cup 10: harm you
- Cup 11: to give you
- Cup 12: a hope
- Cup 13: and a future
- Cup 14: Jeremiah 29:11

Divide the students into two teams. Give each team time to plan what they will build with the cups. They can build a house, a tower, or any other structure. The cups must be used in the order of the verse. Give the teams two minutes to build their structures.

Offering: Plans for Giving

Did you know God wants you to make plans for giving to Him? That's right. God wants us to plan what we will give and then, give it cheerfully.

2 Corinthians 9:7 (NIV) says, "Each of you should give what you have decided in your heart to give, not reluctantly or under compulsion, for God loves a cheerful giver."

So, let's make plans on what we want to give in the offering every week in this new year.

Skit: No Plans

Supplies Needed: lab coat, zany glasses

PROFESSOR CONFUZED: Hello everyone. I am Professor Confuzed. It is so good to see you. I don't have time to talk very long. I am in a hurry.

NARRATOR: Well, hello, Professor Confuzed. It is so good to see you too. I'm so glad you could come to visit today. Why are you in such a hurry?

PROFESSOR: I'm getting married.

NARRATOR: That's wonderful, Professor. Are you getting married today?

PROFESSOR: Yes, I think so. I want a very big wedding with lots of people.

NARRATOR: What do you mean, you *think* you're getting married today?

PROFESSOR: I asked this wonderful girl to marry me yesterday, and she said yes. So, I assume we are getting married today, unless she has something to do and wants to make it tomorrow.

NARRATOR: Professor, didn't your fiancée and you plan *when* you were going to be married?

PROFESSOR: No, we were too busy looking into each other's eyes and telling each other how much we love each other and…

NARRATOR: Professor, I don't think the children want to hear this part.

PROFESSOR: Sorry.

NARRATOR: Professor, I doubt your fiancée is planning to get married today or tomorrow.

PROFESSOR: Oh dear, oh dear. Why doesn't she want to marry me? I am so upset.

NARRATOR: I didn't say she doesn't want to marry you, but when you do something as important as getting married, you have to plan the wedding.

PROFESSOR: I'm confused.

NARRATOR: Yes, you are. For instance, you have to plan when you are getting married. It's all right to get married right away. but you have to get together with your fiancée and decide when.

PROFESSOR: I see what you mean. I'll call her. and we'll decide when. Then we'll have a huge wedding. You are all invited.

NARRATOR: Where?

PROFESSOR: What do you mean, where? To my wedding, of course?

NARRATOR: Where will your wedding take place?

PROFESSOR: At church.

NARRATOR: This church?

PROFESSOR: Yes, this church.

NARRATOR: Who's going to marry you?

PROFESSOR: Her name is Agnes. Ah, Agnes, what a beautiful name?

NARRATOR: I mean, who is going to perform the ceremony?

PROFESSOR: Pastor _____ will. He likes me.

NARRATOR: Did you ask him yet?

PROFESSOR: No, but I'm sure if we show up at the church, he'll marry us.

NARRATOR: Do you have a license?

PROFESSOR: No, I don't drive a car. I'd rather take the bus.

NARRATOR: I'm glad to hear that, but what I meant is a marriage license.

PROFESSOR: You have to have a license to get married? Amazing.

NARRATOR: Professor, getting married takes planning. I think you and Agnes should sit down and plan the wedding. Hopefully she's not as confused as you are.

PROFESSOR: Actually, she is so happy to be marrying someone who has a memory that is so much better than hers. She's just a little forgetful, you know. Just think, soon she will be Mrs. Agnes Confuzed.

NARRATOR: Professor Confuzed, I'm so happy for you and Agnes.

PROFESSOR: I have to go now. I am making my Agnes a wedding cake. It's been in the oven two hours. I think it might be done.

NARRATOR: Oh Professor, you're so confused. I'm sure glad God isn't confused about the plans He has for our lives. He planned every moment before we were ever born.

Verse of the Day: Jeremiah 29:11 *"For I know the plans I have for you," declares the LORD, "plans to prosper you and not to harm you, plans to give you hope and a future."*

Praise and Worship:

Object Lessons:

1. Object Lesson: Building Plans

Use New Year's Slide B.

Today, children, I have a picture of blueprints for a house. Builders use blueprints for every house that they build. These blueprints are the plans for how the house will be built. What do you think would happen if a builder and his crew went out to build a house and didn't follow the blueprints? Give students an opportunity to answer.

Just as there are blueprints for houses, God has a blueprint for our lives. He is the master builder, and He knows before we were ever created what He plans for our lives. If we trust Him, obey Him, and cooperate with Him, He will do great things in us and through us. He has plans for our good.

When I look at these blueprints, I don't see a house. I just see a lot of lines and measurements. When the house is built using these plans, then I'll know what it looks like. I also don't know all the plans God has for me, but God is not finished with me yet. He will build His plans in our lives at the right time.

2. Object Lesson: Resolutions

Supplies needed: long sheet of paper with writing

Show the sheet of paper. *I've been working on my New Year's resolutions this year. What are some of the resolutions people make?* Allow students to answer. Make suggestions if they don't have enough ideas. *What are some of the New Year's resolutions you want to make?* Offer suggestions.

Here are few of mine. Talk about silly resolutions like brush my teeth once a month or eat sometimes. Allow your students to tell you how silly those resolutions are.

There are important resolutions, though. These are resolutions we make to love God, serve Him, and love other people. What are some resolutions we could make? If your students can't think of any, make some suggestions.

God wants us to make resolutions and write them down. Habakkuk 2:2 (NKJV) says, "Then the Lord answered me and said: 'Write the vision And make it plain on tablets, That he may run who reads it.'"

Let's make some God resolutions this year.

Message: The Call (Jeremiah 1:4-10)

Supplies Needed: Job Application

In my hand I have a job application. When a person applies for a job, he has to fill out one of these. Then the employer will look at the application and decide if the person qualifies for the job. One of the questions on this application is age. To have this job, you have to be at least 18 years old.

How old do you think Jeremiah was when God called him to be a prophet? Have the children guess Jeremiah's age. Then read Jeremiah 1:4-10.

We don't know for sure how old Jeremiah was, but we know that he was very young. Young Jewish boys were considered men at age twelve or thirteen, so he was younger than that.

Lots of times, children don't think they can be used by God because they are too young or because they think that they are nobody special. They think they don't have the qualifications for the job God wants them to do. But God has a plan for your life, just as He had a plan for Jeremiah's life when he was young. The only qualifications you need to work for God is salvation and a willing heart. If you are saved and are willing to follow God's plans for your life, here are some things you should know based on Jeremiah 1:

> *God called you before you were even born.*
>
> *He set you apart for His plans.*
>
> *His anointing upon you as children is for NOW.*
>
> *He will give you the words He wants you to say.*

Response:

One plan God has for our lives is for us to worship Him. Let's take time to do that. As you are worshipping, God may show you other plans He has for your lives. Spend some time worshipping, then pray for each student.

About the Author:

Pastor Tamera Kraft has been a children's pastor for over thirty years. She is the director of a ministry called Revival Fire For Kids, where she mentors other children's leaders, teaches workshops, and is a children's ministry consultant and children's revivalist. She is a recipient of the 2007 National Children's Leaders Association Shepherd's Cup for lifetime achievement in children's ministry.

Tamera hosts a children's ministry podcast called IGNITE KIDMIN, available on most podcast providers and provides coaching and resources for IGNITE KIDMIN patron subscribers. Find out more about this at http://revivalfire4kids.com/ignite.

You can find out more about Revival Fire for Kids at http://revivalfire4kids.com.

www.ingramcontent.com/pod-product-compliance
Lightning Source LLC
Chambersburg PA
CBHW081006140626
46546CB00019B/3450